CORNISH
Wit & Humour

TREVOR ITHIC

BRADWELL
BOOKS

Published by Bradwell Books

9 Orgreave Close Sheffield S13 9NP

Email: books@bradwellbooks.co.uk

Compiled by Trevor Ithic

British Library Cataloguing in Publication Data: a catalogue record for
this book is available from the British Library.

1st Edition

ISBN: 9781910551035

Print: Hobbs the Printers, Totton, Hants

Design by: jenksdesign@yahoo.co.uk/07506 471162

Illustrations: ©Tim O'Brien 2014

At a primary school in Penryn the teacher came up with a good problem for her maths class to solve.

"Suppose, there were a dozen sheep and six of them jumped over a fence," she said to the group of seven-year-olds, "How many would be left"

Little Harry, a farmer's son, put his hand up. "None," he answered.

"None?" exclaimed his teacher. "Harry, I'm afraid you don't know your arithmetic."

"Really, Miss?" said Harry, cockily, "And you don't know your sheep. When one goes, they all go!"

Q: What's a Cornishman's idea of a balanced diet?

A: A pint of scrumpy in each hand

A gang of robbers broke into the Truro Lawyers' Club by mistake. The old legal lions put up a fierce fight for their lives and their money. The gang was happy to escape in one piece. "It ain't so bad," one crook said. "At least we got fifty quid between us."

His boss screamed at him, "I warned you to stay clear of lawyers... we had £200 when we broke in!"

At a cricket match in Calstock a fast bowler sent one down and it just clipped the bail. As nobody yelled "Ow's att", the batsman picked up the bail and replaced it. He looked at the umpire and said, "Windy today, int it?"

"Yes," said the umpire, "Mind it doesn't blow your cap off when you're walking back to the pavilion."

Many years ago, a tin miner fell down shaft in the Geevor mine.

The deputy shouted, "Ess anythin' brokun?"
"Naw," he replied, "there's nawthen down 'ere but a few rocks."

Two aerials meet on a roof, fall in love, get married. The ceremony was rubbish - but the reception was brilliant.

A man and his wife walked past Rick Stein's famous fish restaurant in Padstow. "Did you smell that food?" the woman asked. "Wonderful!"

Being the kind-hearted, generous man that he was, her husband thought, "What the hell, I'll treat her!" So they walked past it a second time.

A Cornishman is driving through Devon, when he passes a farmer standing in the middle of a huge field. He pulls the car over and watches the farmer standing stock-still, doing absolutely nothing. Intrigued, the man walks over to the farmer and asks him, "Excuse me sir, but what are you doing?"

The farmer replies, "I'm trying to win a Nobel Prize."
"How?" Asks the puzzled Cornishman.

"Well," says the Devonian, "I heard they give the prize to people who are outstanding in their field."

The owner of a large company in Falmouth went down to check out how everything was going. He notices a young man just relaxing with his feet up in the coffee room. "Just how much are you getting paid a week?" asked the guvnor.

"Two hundred quid!" Replies the young man.

Taking out his wallet, the boss hands him two hundred pounds and says, "Here is a week's pay. Now don't come back!"

A supervisor walks, in with a piece of paper, just as the young man goes out the door. The boss asks him, "How long was that lazy git working here?"

"He doesn't work here," says the supervisor, "He was just waiting for me to give him these directions!"

One day a rich man from Restronguet Point was driving his Mercedes Benz past a field near Redruth and he saw a shabby man standing there chewing grass. The rich man stopped the car and asked the man, "Why are you eating grass"

The man replied, "I am very, very poor and hungry and I have no money to buy food."

The rich man tells him to climb in the car, "Come home with me to Restronguet Point."
The poor man shakes his head and says, "But I can't. I have six children out in this field, all eating grass too."

The rich man says, "That doesn't matter, they're all welcome to come home with me to eat."

So the poor man rounds up his kids and they all get in the Mercedes. The poor man can't thank the rich man enough, "I'm so very grateful, sir."

"That's okay," says the rich man, "You should see the grass in my garden, it must be a foot high."

Q: What do surfers do when they see each other?
A: Wave.

A passenger in a taxi tapped the driver on the shoulder to ask him something.

The driver screamed, lost control of the cab, nearly hit a bus, drove up over the curb and stopped just inches from a large plate glass window.

For a few moments everything was silent in the cab, then the driver said, "Please, don't ever do that again. You scared the daylights out of me."

The passenger, who was also frightened, apologised and said he didn't realise that a tap on the shoulder could frighten him so much, to which the driver replied, "I'm sorry, it's really not your fault at all. Today is my first day driving a cab. I've been driving a hearse for the last twenty-five years."

A group of backpackers from Falmouth University were sitting around a campfire one evening when a stranger asked to join them. Glad to add to their group, they agreed. The evening's fun soon turned to jokes. One of the students started to tell jokes in which Exeter University was the butt of the humour. The stranger who, it turned out, had graduated from Exeter University himself, became more and more furious with each quip. Finally, he had had enough and pulled out his razor and began to threaten the Cornish lads with it. Fortunately for them, he couldn't find a socket to plug it into.

Q: What did King Arthur call it when all his knights changed places around The Round Table?
A: The knight shift

A plain Jane from Penzance goes to see Madame Grizelda, a fortune-teller, and asks about her future love life.

Madame Grizelda tells her, "Two men are madly in love with you – Mark and Maurice."

"Who will be the lucky one?" asks Jane excitedly.

Madame Grizelda answers, "Maurice will marry you, and Mark will be the lucky one."

"You're looking glum," the captain of Bugle C.C. remarked to one of his players.

"Yes, the doctor says I can't play cricket," said the downcast man.

"Really?" replied the captain, "I didn't know he'd ever seen you play?"

Q: What did King Arthur say to the Round Table before bedtime?
A: Knighty Knight

A man from Bude decided to become a monk so he went to the monastery and talked to the head monk.

The head monk said, "You must take a vow of silence and can only say two words every three years."

The man agreed and after the first three years, the head monk came to him and said, "What are your two words?" "Food cold!" the man replied.

Three more years went by and the head monk came to him and said, "What are your two words?" "Robe dirty!" the man exclaimed.

Three more years went by and the head monk came to him and said, "What are your two words?"

"I quit!" said the man.

"Well," the head monk replied, "I'm not surprised. You've done nothing but complain ever since you got here!"

A Penryn man fell out with his in-laws and banned them from entering the house while he was in it. His wife faithfully carried out his wishes until she was on her deathbed and then asked sadly, "Haven't I always been a supportive wife to you, John?"

"Yes, me lover," he replied, "The best."

"Then I would love it if you could grant my last request and let my sister Sarah ride in the first car with you at my funeral?"

"Alright, me lover," he agreed heavily, "But I'm warning you, it'll spoil all me pleasure!"

A tourist from West Virginia is on the Torpoint Ferry crossing into Cornwall for the first time. Upon seeing some seagulls, he says to the man next to him, "Them's darned pretty birds."

The Cornishman says, "Them's gulls."

"Well," says the American, "Gulls or guys, them's darned pretty birds."

"Ayse, I always go to berrins," said an old fishwife from Mousehole when asked if she was going to a neighbour's funeral. 'Tes like this, see, if you don't go the other folks' berrins, they won't come to yourn."

Two council workers on a site in Truro are surveying land they're about to dig up.

The gaffer says to one of them, "You go and get the metal detector and check for pipe work and I'll get the kettle on and have a brew."

The gaffer gets the tea going while his mate starts work. Half-hour later the gaffer puts his paper down, next to his mug of tea, to find out how work is progressing and he finds his mate sitting on a wall scratching his head.

"What's up with you?" The gaffer asks. "There's pipework all over the place. Look!"

The young worker sets off across the land, the bleeper sounding continuously as the detector passes the ground in front of him.

The gaffer watches him, laughing, then he says, "Are you soft or what? You're wearing steel toe caps in your boots!"

At The Red Lion Inn in St. Kew, a newcomer asked an elderly local regular, "Have you lived here all your life, old fellow?"

The old man took a sip of his cider and, after a long pause, replied, "Not yet, me 'ansome!"

There's a man in Covelly who claims to have invented a game that's a bit like cricket; what he doesn't realise is Devon County Cricket Club's been playing it for years.

A local doctor was famous in the Bude area for always catching exceptionally large fish. One day while he was on one of his frequent fishing trips, he was called to a woman in labour at a nearby farm. He rushed to her aid and delivered a healthy baby boy. The farmer had nothing to weigh the baby with so the doctor used his fishing scales - the baby weighed 21 lbs 13 oz.

A man rushed into Royal Cornwall Hospital and asked a nurse for a cure for hiccups. Grabbing a cup of water, the nurse quickly splashed it into the man's face.

"What did you that for?" screamed the man, wiping his face.

"Well, you don't have the hiccups now, do you?" said the nurse. "No," replied the man. "But my wife out in the car does.

Down the King's Head, a group of blokes sit around drinking when a mobile phone on the table rings. One of the men picks up the mobile and puts the speaker-phone on.

A woman's voice says, "How are you, darling? I hope you don't mind but I've just seen a diamond ring priced £2000 and wondered if I can buy it? I've got your credit card with me."

"Of course, my dear, go ahead," answers the man.

"While I'm on," purrs the lady, "I've noticed a top of the range car I'd like. It's only £65,000, could I order that as well?"

"Of course, my angel," replies the man.

His friends around the table look at each other in disbelief as the lady continues, "And I've just noticed a house on the coast at St. Ives, me handsome. It's only £750,000 - could we have that as well please?"

"Of course, sugar," answers the man, without so much as blinking.

The phone call is ended and the man smiles at the others and takes a long swill of beer. Then he looks around and shouts "Anyone know whose phone this is?"

It was match day for the Pirates and excited crowds filled the streets of Penzance, heading for the Mennaye Field. A funeral procession drove slowly through the throng. One of the Pirates supporters stopped, took off his hat and bowed reverently as the hearse passed.

"That was a nice thing to do," remarked his mate.

"Well," said the Pirates fan, "She was a good wife to me for thirty odd years."

"I can't believe it," said the American tourist, looking at the grey skies over St. Ives, "I've been here an entire week and it's done nothing but rain. When do you guys have summer here?"

"Well, that's hard to say," replied the local. "Last year, it was on a Wednesday."

Q: What do you call a Devonian in the 4th Round of the FA Cup?
A: The Referee.

Derek and Duncan were long-time neighbours in Fowey. Every time, Derek saw Duncan coming round to his house, his heart sank. This was because he knew that, as always, Duncan would be visiting him in order to borrow something and he was fed up with it.

"I'm not going to let Duncan get away with it this time," he said quietly to his wife, "Watch what I'm about to do."

"Hi there, I wondered if you were thinking about using your hedge trimmer this afternoon?" asked Duncan.

"Oh, I'm very sorry," said Derek, trying to look apologetic, "but I'm actually going to be using it all afternoon."

"In that case," replied Duncan with a big grin, "You won't be using your golf clubs, will you? Mind if I borrow them?"

Two Callington Cricket Club players are chatting in the bar after a match. "So did you have a hard time explaining last week's game to the wife?" says one.

"I certainly did," says the other, "She found out I wasn't there!"

A farmer near St. Agnes saw a stranger drinking from his stream. He shouts, "Wozzon! Ee den wanna be drinkin' dat, It'is fulla horse pee an' cow doings."

"Oh hi there. I'm your new neighbour from London," says the stranger, "I've just bought a cute little cottage in the village. I'm not used to the way you chaps speak, so can you say that again a bit slower, please?"

The farmer replies, "If - you -use - two - hands - you - won't - spill – any."

Three Cornish women are talking in a bar about a party they've been invited to.

The first one says, "We've got to all wear an item that matches something belonging to our husbands at this party, haven't we?"

"Yeah," said the other two, "But what?"

The first one continued, "Well, my husband's got black hair and I've got a little black dress I can diet into by then."

The second one says, "That's a good idea. My husband has got brown hair and I've got a brown dress I can diet into by then too."

The third one looks a bit hesitant and says, "I just need to go on a diet - my husband's bald!"

Two mums are watching their teenage sons go off to school in Newquay. One kid is sulking and dragging his feet; the other is skipping along happily.

"I wish I could get Ben to go to school willingly," said one mum. "Try telling him the surf's going to be low," said the other grinning.

Darren proudly drove his new convertible into Truro and parked it on the main street. He was on his way to the recycling centre to get rid of an unwanted gift, a foot spa, which he left on the back seat.

He had walked half way down the street when he realised that he had left the top down with the foot spa still in the back.

He ran all the way back to his car, but it was too late...another five foot spas had been dumped in the car.

Two elderly ladies in St. Keverne had been friends for many decades. Over the years, they had shared all kinds of fun but of late their activities had been limited to meeting a few times a week to play cards. One day, they were playing pontoon when one looked at the other and said, "Now don't get mad at me, me lover. I know we've been friends for a long time but I just can't think of your name. I've thought and thought, but I can't remember it. Please tell me what your name is." Her friend got a bit teasy and, for at least three minutes, she just stared and glared at her. Finally she said, "How soon do you need to know?"

Ten women out on a hen night in Falmouth thought it would be sensible if one of them stayed more sober than the other nine and looked after the money to pay for their drinks. After deciding who would hold the money, they all put twenty pounds into the kitty to cover expenses. At closing time after a few spritzers, several vodka and cokes, and a Pina Colada each, they stood around deciding how to divvy up the leftover cash. "How do we stand?" said Sharon.

"Stand?!" said Debbie. "That's the easy part! I'm wondering how I can walk. I've missed the last bus to Budock Water!"

A lawyer at Truro Crown Court says to the judge, "Your Honour, I wish to appeal my client's case on the basis of newly discovered evidence."

His Lordship replies, "And what is the nature of the new evidence?"

The lawyer says, "My Lord, I discovered that my client still has £500 left."

Q: What was Camelot famous for?
A: It's knight life

One afternoon at Penwith College, a group of sixth-formers were attending one of their first classes in psychology. The topic was emotional extremes.

"Let's begin by discussing some contrasts," said the tutor. He pointed to a student in the front row, "What is the opposite of joy?"

The student thought about it briefly, then answered "Sadness." The tutor asked another student, "What is the opposite of depression?"

She paused then said, "Elation."

"And you," the tutor said to another student sitting at the back, "What about the opposite of woe?"

The student thought for a moment, then replied, "Um, I believe that would be 'giddy up'."

A man walks into the fishmongers in Port Isaac carrying a halibut under his arm. "Do you make fishcakes?" he asks.

"Of course," says the fishmonger.

"Oh good," says the man. "It's his birthday."

Albert, an extremely wealthy 65 year-old, arrives at Carlyon Bay Golf Club with a beautiful 25-year-old blonde on his arm

His buddies at the club are all aghast. They corner him and ask, "Albert, how did you get the trophy girlfriend?"

"Girlfriend!" exclaims, Albert, "She's my wife!"

His friends are shocked, but continue to ask, "So, how'd you persuade her to marry you?" Albert replies, "I lied about my age."

His friends respond, "What do you mean? Did you tell her you were only 50?"

Albert smiles and says, "No, I told her I was 81."

In the staff canteen at Falmouth Docks, Jack was always showing Bob photos of his dog and saying how clever it was: doing tricks, playing ball, bringing his newspaper and slippers. One day Jack brought in the album from his daughter's wedding so Bob could look through the photos. Bob decided to tease Jack a little and said, "Hang on, where's your precious dog? I'm surprised he wasn't the Best Man!"

Jack looked at Bob as if he was stupid, "Don't be silly, someone had to take the photos."

A woman walked into the kitchen to find her husband stalking around with a fly swatter. "What are you doing?" She demanded.

"Hunting flies," he replied.

"Oh. Killed any?" She asked.

"Yep, three males and two females," he replied.

Intrigued, she said, "How can you tell?"

"Three were on a beer can, and two were on the phone." he replied.

A pupil at a school in Bude asked his teacher, "Are 'trousers' singular or plural?"

The teacher replied, "They're singular on top and plural on the bottom."

In a school in Camelford, a little boy just wasn't getting good marks. One day, his teacher was checking his homework and said, "Lee, once again I'm afraid I can only give you two out of ten."

Little Lee looked up at her and said, "Well, Miss, I don't want to scare you, but…"

He stopped, a worried expression on his face.

"What is it? Tell me, Lee," said his teacher kindly.

"Well," said the boy, "my daddy says if I don't get better marks soon, somebody is going to get a spanking."

A police officer arrived at the scene of a major pile up on the A30.

The officer runs over to the front car and asks the driver, "Are you seriously hurt?"

The driver turns to the officer and says, "How the heck should I know? Do I look like a lawyer?"

Two drunken surfers are in a pub in Polzeath when one of them asks, "Hey man, what's worst: ignorance or indifference?" The other guy answers, "I really don't know and I really don't care."

A man walks into a bank in Wadebridge and says to the female assistant at the counter, "I want to open a bank account now!"

To which the lady replied, "I beg your pardon, sir, what did you say?"

"Listen cloth-ears," snapped the man aggressively, "I said I want to open a bank account right now."

"Sir, I'm sorry but we do not tolerate rudeness to staff in this bank!"

The clerk left the window and went over to the bank manager and complained to him about her customer. They both returned and the manager asked, "What seems to be the problem here?"

"There's no problem," the man said, "I just won 50 million in the lottery and I want to open a bank account in this bank right now!"

"I see, sir," the manager said, "and this silly old cow is giving you a hard time?"

A tourist, loaded with expensive fishing rods and equipment, approaches an old fisherman sitting on the bank of the River Lynher.

"I say, old man," says the emmet, "Is this river any good for fish?" "It must be," said the Cornishman, "I can't get any of them to leave it."

A police officer sees a man driving around Launceston with a pickup truck full of otters. He pulls the man over and says, "You can't drive around with otters in this town! There's a wildlife centre in North Petherwin, take them there immediately." The man says "OK, officer" and drives away.

The next week, the officer sees the man still driving around with the truck full of otters, and they're all wearing sunglasses. He pulls the man over and says crossly, "I thought I told you to take those otters to the Tamar Otter and Wildlife Centre last week?" The man replies, "I did and they loved it, so today I'm taking them to the beach at Carbis Bay."

Two surfers are getting ready to paddle out.

Surfer one says, "Hey, guess what! I got a new long-board for my wife!"

Surfer two says, "Good swop!"

Sam worked in a telephone marketing company in Truro. One day he walked into his boss's office and said, "I'll be honest with you, I know the economy isn't great, but I have three companies after me, and, with respect, I would like to ask for a pay rise."

After a few minutes of haggling, his manager finally agreed to a 5% pay rise, and Sam happily got up to leave.

"By the way," asked the boss as Sam went to the door, "Which three companies are after you?"

"The electric company, the water company, and the phone company," Sam replied.

A farmer was driving along a country road near the picturesque village of Sennen Cove with a large load of fertiliser. A little boy, playing in front of his cottage, saw him and called out, "What do you have on your truck?"

"Fertiliser," the farmer replied

"What are you going to do with it?" asked the little boy. "Put it on strawberries," answered the farmer.

"You ought to live here," the little boy advised him. "We put sugar and cream on ours."

It was a quiet night in Hayle and a man and his wife were fast asleep, when there was an unexpected knock on the door. The man looked at his alarm clock. It was half past three in the morning. "I'm not getting out of bed at this time," he thought and rolled over.

There was another louder knock.

"Aren't you going to answer that?" asked his wife irritably.

So the man dragged himself out of bed and went downstairs. He opened the door to find a strange man standing outside. It didn't take the homeowner long to realise the man was totally drunk.

"All right, me 'ansome?" slurred the stranger. "Can you give me a push?"

"No, I'm sorry I most certainly can't. It's half past three in the morning and I was in bed," said the man and he slammed the front door.

He went back up to bed and told his wife what happened. "That wasn't very nice of you," she said. "Remember that night we broke down in the pouring rain on the way to pick the kids up from the babysitter, and you had to knock on that man's door to get us started again? What would have happened if he'd told us to get lost?"

"But the man who just knocked on our door was as drunk as a perraner," replied her husband.

"Well, we can at least help move his car somewhere safe and sort him out a taxi," said his wife. "He needs our help."

So the husband got out of bed again, got dressed, and went downstairs. He opened the door, but couldn't to see the stranger anywhere so he shouted, "Hey, do you still want a push?"

In answer, he heard a voice call out, "Yes please!"

So, still unable to see the stranger, he shouted, "Where are you?" "I'm over here, me 'ansome," the stranger replied, "on your swing."

Everyday a lady walks past a pet shop in Helston on her way to work. One day she notices a parrot in the window and stops to admire the bird. The parrot says to her, "How are you, maid? You're as fat as a pudding."

Well, the lady is furious! She storms off but on her way back from work she passes the same parrot and, when it sees her, the bird says, "How are you, maid? You're as fat as a pudding."

She is incredibly angry now so she goes to the manager and threatens to sue the pet shop. She demands to have the bird put down. The manager apologises profusely and promises that the bird won't say it again. The next day, she walks past the parrot and, when it sees her, it says, "How are you, maid?"

The woman stops, scowls and with an icy stare, says, "Yes?"
The parrot struts back and forth on its perch in a cocky manner, gawping at her, then it says, "You know."

The president of the Polperro Vegetarian Society really couldn't control himself any more. He simply had to try some pork, just to see what it tasted like. So one day he told his members he was going away for a short break. He left town and headed to a restaurant in Looe. He sat down, ordered a roasted pig, and waited impatiently for his treat. After only a few minutes, he heard someone call his name, and, to his horror, he saw one of his members walking towards him. At exactly the same moment, the waiter arrived at his table, with a huge platter, holding a whole roasted pig with an apple in its mouth. "Isn't this place something?" said the president, thinking quickly, "Look at the way they serve apples!"

Phil's nephew came to him with a problem. "I have my choice of two women," he said, with a worried frown, "A beautiful, penniless young girl whom I love dearly, and a rich widow who I don't really love."

"Follow your heart," Phil counselled, "marry the girl you love."
"Very well, Uncle Phil," said the nephew, "That's sound advice. Thank you."

"You're welcome," replied Phil with a smile, "By the way, where does the widow live?"

Sir Lancelot was hurrying home to Tintagel on a cold, wet night when, suddenly, his purebred Arab stallion suffered a major coronary and dropped dead on the spot. All Sir Lancelot could do was collect up his belongings and tramp onwards through the darkness.

After a few miles he spotted the light of a farmhouse. He strode up the path and banged on the door, shouting, "A horse! A horse! I must have a horse!"

The door opened to reveal a young girl. She looked at Sir Lancelot and said, "Your pardon, good knight, but my father and brothers are out on Bodmin Moor and will not be back before noon tomorrow. They are riding all our horses."

Sir Lancelot was saddened by this and said, "But I must return home immediately. Have you any idea where I may acquire alternative transportation?"

The young girl said, "I know of no other horses hereabouts, but sometimes my brothers ride our Great Dane dog when the need arises. Would that help?"

Sir Lancelot was desperate and said, "If I must, I must. Show me the animal."

The young girl led the way around to the back of the farmhouse to a stable. She disappeared inside and returned leading an enormous dog quite big enough to carry a man. Unfortunately, the dog had seen better days: its coat was threadbare, its legs spindly. It was breathing laboriously.

Sir Lancelot looked at the young girl and said, "Surely, you wouldn't send a knight out on a dog like this?"

The nervous young batsman playing for Gulval C.C. was having a very bad day. In a quiet moment in the game, he muttered to the one of his team-mates, "Well, I suppose you've seen worse players."

There was no response...so he said it again, "I said 'I guess you've seen worse players'."

His team-mate looked at him and answered, "I heard you the first time. I was just trying to think..."

A farmer from the Okehampton once visited a farmer based near St. Just. The visitor asked, "How big is your farm?" to which the Cornish farmer replied, "Can you see those trees over there? That's the boundary of my farmland."

"Is that all?" said the Devonian farmer, "It takes me three days to drive to the boundary of my farm."

The Cornishman looked at him and said, "I had a car like that once."

One day at the Royal Cornwall Hospital, a group of primary school children were being given a tour. A nurse showed them the x-ray machines and asked them if they had ever had broke a bone.

One little boy raised his hand, "I did!"

"Did it hurt?" the nurse asked.

"No!" he replied.

"Wow, you must be a very brave boy!" said the nurse. "What did you break?"

"My sister's arm!"

A woman from Landewednack called Lindy was still not married at thirty-five and she was getting really tired of going to family weddings especially because her old Aunt Maud always came over and said, "You're next!"

It made Lindy so annoyed she racked her brains to figure out how to get Aunt Maud to stop. Sadly, an old uncle died and there was a big family funeral. Lindy spotted Aunt Maud in the crematorium, walked over, pointed at the coffin and said, with a big smile, "You're next!"

At a school in Redruth, the maths teacher poses a question to little Wayne, "If I give £500 to your dad on 12% interest per annum, what will I get back after two years."

"Nothing," says Wayne.

"I am afraid you know nothing about maths, Wayne," says the teacher crossly.

"I am afraid too, sir," replies Wayne, "You don't know nothing about my father."

A woman got on a bus to Falmouth holding a baby. The bus driver said, "That's the ugliest baby I've ever seen!"

In a huff, the woman slammed down her fare and took an aisle seat near the rear of the bus. The man seated next to her sensed that she was agitated and asked her what was wrong. "The bus driver insulted me," she fumed.

The man sympathised with her and said, "Why, he's a public servant and shouldn't say things to insult passengers."

"You're right," she said. "I think I'll go back up there and give him a piece of my mind."

"That's a good idea," the man said. "I'll hold your monkey for you."

A bookdealer in Lostwithiel has discovered the manuscripts for some unpublished, unexpectedly modern sequels by famous Cornish writers including Daphne Du Maurier's *My Cousin Rachel's Second Home* and William Golding's *Lord of the Flies from Newquay.*

An expectant father rang the Treliske Maternity Unit to see how his wife, who had gone into labour, was getting on. By mistake, he was connected to the county cricket ground. "How's it going?" he asked.

"Fine," came the answer, "We've got three out and hope to have the rest out before lunch. The last one was a duck."

In the early days of television sets the ritual of switching the TV on and waiting for the valves to warm up was all part of building the excitement to watch a programme: usually the one that was on! In Newlyn, an old fisherman, Elijah Tregorran decided to tell his neighbour about his newly-acquired television and how he was going to watch the Queen's Coronation. "I've gotta go in now to watch the spectacle," he said, looking at his pocket watch.

His neighbour looked and said, "But it ain't on fer another three hours."

"I knaw," said Jimmy, "but they bin sayin' there'll be a lot there and I want to get a good seat!

Did you hear about the last wish of the henpecked husband of a house-proud wife?

He asked to have his ashes scattered on the carpet.

A golfer was going around the Tregenna Castle Golf and Country Club course. He was talking to his caddy between holes about a forthcoming competition. "I've been drawn against Jack Penhaligon from Newquay, is he any good?"

The caddy checked for a moment and said, "He's absolutely rubbish. Can't get around the course with any ease. He set a new course record for the worst round ever that has only just been beaten."

"Oh, I should easily get through to the next round then, shan't I?" said the golfer complacently.

The caddy looked down at the scorecard and said, "I wouldn't bet on it!"

A young knight meets Merlin by Tintagel Castle and says, "You're Merlin aren't you?"

"Why yes," says Merlin, smoothing his long white beard. "It's nice to be recognised!" "You're a bit of a Wizard, I hear?" says the young knight.

"Well, yes. I've been told I'm skilled," says Merlin modestly.

"You do tricks and things, don't you?" says the young knight. "Magical stuff?"

Merlin nods. "Magical, yes, that's correct."

"You can turn kings into frogs and that sort of thing? Is that right?"

Merlin nods again. "Well, yes. I suppose I could turn a king into a frog."

The young knight looks thoughtful. "Have you ever mucked up? You know, made a mistake?"

"Well, yes," replies Merlin, "hasn't everyone?"

"Can you reverse a curse?" asks the young knight.

"Yes, I can," says Merlin confidently, "with knowledge of who applied the Curse and the actual words of enchantment, I could do it. Why?"

The young knight looks miserable and wretched. "I'm accursed!"
"Really?" says Merlin, "and how long have you been bewitched?"
"Years," replies the young knight.

"Do you remember the exact words spoken over you to lay this curse?" asks Merlin.

"Yes!" exclaims the unhappy knight, "I can't forget them!"

Merlin lays a comforting hand on his shoulder. "Tell me, son. What were they?"

With a quaver in his voice, the young knight replies, "Do you take this woman to be your lawful-wedded wife?"

Three blondes were walking in near the Cutkive Woods when they came upon a set of tracks.

The first blonde said, "Those are deer tracks."

The second blonde said, "No, those are horse tracks."

The third blonde said, "You're both wrong, those are cattle tracks."

The Blondes were still arguing when the 11.45 train to Liskeard hit them.

Anne and Matt, a Polzeath couple, went to the Royal Cornwall Show and found a weighing scale that tells your fortune and weight.

"Hey, listen to this," said Matt, showing his wife a small white card. "It says I'm bright, energetic, and a great husband."

"Yeah," Anna said, "And it has your weight wrong as well."

Two men were walking through the Heligan Woods when a large tiger that had escaped from Newquay Zoo walked out into the clearing no more than 50 feet in front of them. The first man dropped his backpack and dug out a pair of running shoes, then began to furiously attempt to lace them up as the tiger slowly approached them. The second man looked at him confused, and said, "What are you doing, me 'ansome? Running shoes aren't going to help. You can't outrun that tiger."

"I don't need to," said the first man, "I just need to outrun you."

An old chap from Newlyn went to the G.P.

"Doctor," says the old boy, "I am sweating buckets and I feel right beheemed."

"Flu?" asks the doc.

"No," says the old chap, "I rode here on me bike like I always do."

A Hurrah Henry from Exeter was driving around St. Austell in his fancy new BMW and realised that he was lost. The driver stopped a local character, old Tom, and said, "Hey, you there! Old man, what happens if I turn left here?"

"Dawn't knaw, sir," replied Tom.

"Well, what if I turn right here - where will that take me?" continued the visitor.

"Dawn't knaw, sir," replied old Tom.

Becoming exasperated, the driver continued, "Well, what if I go straight on?"

A flicker of knowledge passed over old Tom's face but then he replied, "Dawn't knaw, sir."

"I say, old man, you don't know a lot do you?" retorted the posh bloke.

Old Tom looked at him and said, "I may not knaw a lot, sir, but I ain't lost like what you are!"

With that, old Tom walked off leaving the motorist stranded.

Three sisters aged 92, 94 and 96 live in a house together in Nancegollan. One night the 96 year-old draws a bath. She puts her foot in and pauses. She yells to the other sisters, "Were I getting in or out of the bath, me lover?"

The 94 year-old hollers back, "I don't know. I'll come up and see." She starts up the stairs but then she pauses, "Were I going upstairs or down, me lover?"

The 92 year-old is sitting at the kitchen table having tea listening to her sisters. She shakes her head and says, "I hope I never gets that forgetful, knock on wood." She raps on the oak table loudly. Then she shouts upstairs, "I'll come up and help the pair of you as soon as I see who's at the door."